LIES,
TRUTHS,
& MYTHS
ABOUT BRACES
& INVISALIGN

DR. BRYAN P. NELSON DDS, MS

LIES,
TRUTHS,
& *MYTHS*
ABOUT BRACES
& INVISALIGN

**WHAT YOUR ORTHODONTIST
MAY OR MAY NOT WANT
YOU TO KNOW**

Advantage.

Published by Advantage, Charleston, South Carolina.
Member of Advantage Media Group.

ADVANTAGE is a registered trademark, and the Advantage colophon is a trademark of Advantage Media Group, Inc.

Printed in the United States of America.

10 9 8 7 6 5 4 3 2 1

ISBN: 978-1-64225-045-9

Cover design by Mary Hamilton.
Layout design by Matthew Morse.

This publication is designed to provide accurate and authoritative information in regard to the subject matter covered. It is sold with the understanding that the publisher is not engaged in rendering legal, accounting, or other professional services. If legal advice or other expert assistance is required, the services of a competent professional person should be sought.

Advantage Media Group is proud to be a part of the Tree Neutral® program. Tree Neutral offsets the number of trees consumed in the production and printing of this book by taking proactive steps such as planting trees in direct proportion to the number of trees used to print books. To learn more about Tree Neutral, please visit **www.treeneutral.com**.

Advantage Media Group is a publisher of business, self-improvement, and professional development books and online learning. We help entrepreneurs, business leaders, and professionals share their Stories, Passion, and Knowledge to help others Learn & Grow. Do you have a manuscript or book idea that you would like us to consider for publishing? Please visit **advantagefamily.com** or call **1.866.775.1696**.

To Dr. Blanca Lares-Nelson and Kyan and Khiana Nelson, my amazing family, for putting up with me and loving me, and Dr. Donald Schmitz, the orthodontist who convinced me to be an orthodontist in the first place.

Contents

INTRODUCTION 1
What Your Orthodontist
Doesn't Want You to Know

CHAPTER ONE 9
Why Getting Your Teeth Fixed
Should Be Easier Than Ever

CHAPTER TWO 19
All Doctors Are Not Equal

CHAPTER THREE 27
The Earlier, the Better
Is Not Always True

CHAPTER FOUR 39
All Braces Are Not Equal

CHAPTER FIVE 53

How to Have the Best
Orthodontic Experience

CHAPTER SIX 61

What Patients Need to Do

CHAPTER SEVEN 75

Good Teeth Are Key to Success
and Happiness—Really!

SUMMARY 81

The Dos and Don'ts of Orthodontics

EPILOGUE 87

My Approach to Orthodontics

What Your Orthodontist Doesn't Want You to Know

After a couple of decades in orthodontic practice, I started to feel like some of the grumpy old doctors among my teachers in dental school. I always used to wonder why they were so unhappy. Then I started getting grumpy myself. But I wasn't grumpy because of my work—I was grumpy for you, the patient. By which, I mean I got irritated with the way some orthodontists treat their patients. The three things that irritate me most are:

- There are many orthodontists doing procedures that are not based on any research results that prove they work, but they are costing patients a lot of money.

- There are many orthodontists starting orthodontic treatment on children, *sometimes as young as five years old,* who don't need it—at great expense for their parents—and, again, without proven long-term success.

- There are many orthodontists who are not keeping up with the new approaches that make having braces much more pleasant, that work more effectively, and that take less time—and by not keeping up, they're costing their patients time, money, and discomfort.

You can see why I'm grumpy and frustrated about orthodontics today—and I hope it bothers you as much as it does me.

In my opinion, the orthodontic profession has ceased to be the completely honorable profession it once was, and which I expected it to be—and patients certainly hope it will be. When you take your child in, for example, you're hoping that the orthodontist is doing what's in the best interest of your child, not trying to invent some reason why you need to drop five grand to do braces immediately, when there's no real need.

But even after I got frustrated about all of this, it took me a while to decide to write a book. I *wanted* to tell the truth about how orthodontics is being practiced by many doctors today, but I was afraid of the backlash from my colleagues. Nobody wants to be unpopular among his colleagues, and I knew for certain that I would be courting trouble by revealing some of the things being done in orthodontics today. I also wanted to make sure that I was right in my opinion. I really thought long and hard before I started this book. But I truly feel the public needs to be aware of what is going on because it is just not right, or fair to the patients.

Finally, I couldn't keep quiet any longer. I saw too many patients, children and adults, suffering with orthodontic procedures and appliances that weren't necessary and that cost *a lot* of money. My colleagues were doing great, but their patients were not.

Perhaps I'm particularly sensitive about not doing orthodontic treatment unless absolutely necessary—and about using the most comfortable appliances possible—because, many years ago, I went through a bit of orthodontic hell myself. Not long after I got out of orthodontic residency, I started orthodontic treatment on myself. I had what's called a pendulum appliance put in. It covered the roof of my mouth and had little wires that stuck out the back and attached to my back molars. The purpose of the appliance was to push my upper-right back molars into the correct position. This would fix my bite and make more room for my crooked teeth. Little did I know at that time that my orthodontist was a sadist. Did I mention that I did my own treatment? I

Finally, I couldn't keep quiet any longer. I saw too many patients, children and adults, suffering with orthodontic procedures and appliances that weren't necessary and that cost a lot of money.

am still in therapy over that, decades later. Okay, I'm not really in therapy, but it *was* traumatizing when it happened.

While I was wearing this appliance, my wife and I took a long weekend trip to Puerto Vallarta, and I was on the plane, happily eating snacks. Unfortunately, the wires on the appliance in my mouth had little round coil springs built into them, and, bizarrely, my tongue actually got stuck in one of those coil springs. And I mean stuck! My natural reflex was to pull my tongue out of the spring, and before I could stop myself the spring ripped it open—a big, gaping tear in my tongue. The pain was incredible, the amount of blood was astounding, and my tongue started to swell tremendously.

Luckily, my wife is a dentist, too, so she managed to help me by shaking her head in disbelief, which did not stop the bleeding or do anything for the pain. When we got to Puerto Vallarta, my wife insisted that we stop at the first pharmacy we could find and get a small bottle of lidocaine anesthetic to dab onto the wound. Now, there was that doctor wife I needed! When we got to the pharmacy, the smallest bottle they had was about a one-quart-size glass bottle—and, believe me, I took it. The pain was excruciating.

We took the bottle to our hotel, but as we were opening the door to our room, I felt the bag I was carrying suddenly feel light. The bottle had broken through the bottom of the thin plastic bag, and I saw it falling in slow motion toward the tile floor as I felt this guttural groan from deep inside me saying "Nooooooooo," and then it exploded on the hallway floor tiles. I was frantic. This can't be happening, I thought, WTF! (Wow, that's fantastic!) But my little accident wasn't going to stop me from getting some of that lidocaine. I sprinted into the bathroom to retrieve a glass from the counter and we scooped as much of it as we could from large pieces of the broken bottle into the glass. I got about a tablespoon. Just enough that I could use a Q-tip to apply it to my tongue. That precious tablespoon of anesthetic saved my vacation. By the time I was back on the plane and headed home, my tongue had started to heal. So crazy.

Then, to top it all off, that appliance that had ripped out a piece of my tongue *didn't even work to correct my bite!* After three years of trying all different kinds of appliances and having none of them work, I actually ended up removing a premolar tooth on the side where the appliance had been. Then it took me another two years to finally get that space all closed up. It ended up being one nightmare after another that lasted five years.

Such are the hazards of orthodontic appliances. I admit that this was an extreme situation, but the experience made me determined to make orthodontic treatments work as fast, comfortably, precisely, predictably, and inexpensively as possible for my patients.

But that does not seem to be the attitude of many of my colleagues, so I've written this book to protect you against thoughtless, unscrupulous, or just plain ignorant orthodontists. You need to know what to watch out for. You need to know enough about how orthodontics works so that you can ask the right questions and get answers that will make you an informed consumer. I want you to be able to avoid being taken advantage of. And you need to realize that *you're in charge.* No orthodontist or dentist can—or should—do work on you or your child that you don't want

> *I've written this book to protect you against thoughtless, unscrupulous, or just plain ignorant orthodontists.*

them to do. After reading his book, you'll know better when to say yes and when to say no.

A lot of doctors just don't stay up-to-date on the best ways to do things—ways that can shorten treatment times, decrease discomfort, and save their patients money. Orthodontists are really no different than other human beings and, basically, human beings are lazy. They don't want to do any more than they have to. Sometimes, the higher up you get in your education level, the lazier you get, because you're so focused on your profession. You spent so much time and energy developing your expertise as a doctor that, once you have it, you just want to ride it out until you're ready to retire.

Also, thinking outside of the box is not encouraged in dental school. We are taught there was a right way to do things—and that was it. Master it here, end of story. Due to this mind-set, most doctors are not that willing to further their education continually. Each state has mandatory, annual continuing education requirements in order to maintain licensure, and most doctors barely meet those minimal requirements for continuing education every year. That's why they had to put those requirements in place—because doctors weren't keeping up with the latest technology. The states had to force them to do it.

I've tried to keep up. Over two and a half decades of working in orthodontics—owning my own practice and treating thousands of patients—I have seen numerous techniques for aligning teeth come and go. I've also seen a lot of patients go through plenty of grief dealing with the devices those techniques employed. In the late 1990s, however, Invisalign clear aligners came along, and I liked them right away. They were less obtrusive, patients found them easier to use, and they worked. I started using them on my patients immediately and quickly became the largest user in the state of Colorado—for one thing, I didn't want anybody to have to go through something like I'd been through.

Within the last five years, Invisalign has *really* stepped up its game. The refined, computer-assisted approach they've introduced has, I believe, revolutionized the process of orthodontic treatment. I can use Invisalign aligners for people of any age to fix an amazing variety of orthodontic problems. For that reason, I've become an expert on Invisalign, and I want patients to know just how convenient and effective that approach is. It is truly amazing—faster, more convenient, more effective, and possibly cheaper than previous methods. It's hard to argue with that—and it's a wonder to me that all orthodontists don't use it.

As I said, the profit motive prevents many orthodontists from doing their work in the way that's best for you or your children. A lot of orthodontists will actually match the duration of the treatment to the payments of the fee. Let's say they want to get a fee of $5,000. They find out you can afford a $100 a month payment, so they drag out your treatment to as close to fifty months as possible, so that they can get all of their $5,000. Instead of just trying to be as efficient as possible with the treatment, they adjust for the fee. They also nickel-and-dime you throughout the treatment to get as much money out of you as they possibly can.

In the next chapter, I'll explain to you why orthodontic work today ought to be more convenient, more comfortable, faster, and more effective than it has ever been. Orthodontics has come a long way over its history, and especially in recent years, and the better you understand what *can* be done, the better you'll be able to get the best possible treatment for yourself or your child.

KEEP THIS IN MIND

- I see too many of my fellow orthodontists doing expensive procedures that have not been proven effective, wasting their patients' time and money.

- I have a particular distaste for the all-too-common practice of putting braces and other appliances on children who still have most of their baby teeth, who very rarely require such work.

- I've become a big proponent of Invisalign clear plastic aligners because they offer my patients the best results, the best value, and the least trouble.

CHAPTER ONE

Why Getting Your Teeth Fixed Should Be Easier Than Ever

We are fortunate to live in an era when orthodontic work is—or should be—faster and easier on the patient than it has ever been. Those are the qualities you should be looking for in the work of any orthodontist you consider going to. My sole purpose in writing this book is to give you the information you need to figure out which orthodontist is going to make the work you have done on your teeth faster, easier, less expensive, and actually necessary.

Orthodontics has been practiced since ancient Egypt, when, believe it or not, they tied reeds around teeth to move the teeth into place. They would tie dried papyrus threads around the teeth

> *We are fortunate to live in an era when orthodontic work is—or should be— faster and easier on the patient than it has ever been.*

they wanted to move and when the threads got wet from saliva, they shrank, thus applying force to the teeth to make them move. Pretty ingenious. Yes, even back then, people were apparently concerned about how their teeth looked. Although, of course, there were likely also functional reasons to move teeth as well, such as bite alignment and TMJ (jaw joint) problems.

But we've come a long way since then—and even over the last couple decades—so getting your teeth fixed ought to take a lot less time and trouble than ever before, if orthodontists would just be willing to take advantage of the amazing technologies available today, as well as change how they think. The contrast between the old technologies and the new ones is like the difference between analog and digital in electronic devices—it's revolutionary.

The Limits of Traditional Braces

Let's look at how orthodontics has changed in recent history. Orthodontics has been around in the US for more than a hundred years. It was the first dental specialty recognized by the American Dental Association. Oddly, modern orthodontics has only very recently become significantly different from what it was in the beginning.

Throughout history, people have been developing little devices or appliances that use wires or springs or the like to put pressure on the teeth and move them into a desired position. Then, slowly but surely, people started trying to find better ways to attach things onto teeth to have better control of tooth movement. Eventually they developed metal bands that would fit around the crown of the tooth with little welded attachments, so they could attach wires to them. Putting these bands on was very difficult, because teeth touch each other, or are very close together, and orthodontists were forcing these metal bands around the teeth—quite honestly, hammering these things into place around the teeth. When you have two adjacent teeth and someone is wedging metal between them, you can imagine the excruciating pain that would cause. These days, there are tiny rubber bands or wires that are placed between the teeth where they contact that then push the teeth apart to make space for the bands. These, coincidentally, are called "separators." They still hurt like crazy.

Teeth have traditionally been moved using a wire that is attached to the teeth with small squares with a slot in the middle for the wire to fit into. These little squares are called brackets. Originally, the brackets were attached to those metal bands I just talked about, because they didn't have the amazing bonding agents to affix the brackets directly to the teeth, as we have now—which was an important advance in the design of braces from a comfort and precision standpoint. (Believe it or not, some orthodontists *still* put metal bands around the entire tooth—a difficult and painful process that really isn't necessary anymore.)

The wire that attaches to the brackets is adjusted by the orthodontist to move the teeth. These adjustments require bending the wire in individual spots for each tooth that has to be moved, so each tooth moves in the direction it's supposed to go. This is a slow, painful, and expensive process. The investment of money, time, and pain is daunting for patients.

In the early days, due to the stiffness of the wires used on braces, patients needed to be seen every two to four weeks to have their braces adjusted and to keep the teeth moving. With the advent of new-age metals such as nickel titanium, known as memory wire, the braces don't have to be adjusted as frequently and the forces applied to the teeth are less intense, decreasing the amount of pain associated with the treatment. Today, appointments during certain stages of treatment with traditional braces can be as far apart as twelve to sixteen weeks.

One problem with traditional braces is that, in order for teeth to be moved, the wires need to slide easily through the slots in the brackets attached to a patient's teeth. Friction between the wire and the bracket slows the movement of the teeth and requires the orthodontist to apply heavier forces to move them. In some cases, this heavier force could damage the teeth or make the roots shorter, which is called "root resorption."

Recently, self-ligating (SL) brackets have been developed that may have lower friction (although, to be honest, it's really just a theory, because there is no good evidence that they really *do* reduce the friction clinically and, therefore, reduce overall treatment time), but the friction is still there as a limiting factor in the ease and swiftness of tooth movement. I have used these brackets from the largest and most famous manufacturer of them, and I did not see any benefits to them. I am skeptical that it is more of a marketing ploy than a true breakthrough in bracket technology. We will see if any legitimate clinical research shows up.

That's one of the reasons that traditional orthodontic treatments take such a long time—this lack of precision, even in the most high-tech traditional braces that we have now.

Another thing that happens with traditional braces is that we actually introduce what orthodontists call "iatrogenic tooth movement"—which refers to wrong or incorrect tooth movements—into the treatment. This is because every patient who gets orthodontic treatment has *some* teeth that are in their ideal position already, along with the ones that are *not* in their ideal position. When you put on traditional braces, the wire connects *all* of the teeth, which introduces tension throughout the mouth, so all of the teeth move. Even the teeth that are in great positions when we start are forced to move, and they move into *incorrect* positions. So, as the last step of the treatment, we have to move those teeth *back* into their correct positions. That's one of the reasons that traditional orthodontic treatments take such a long time—this lack of precision, even in the most high-tech traditional braces that we have now.

The most high-tech traditional braces are called "fully customizable," but even they aren't exact. They're much better than what we had before, because they use computer modeling, but going from the computer screen, where you design your custom braces, to actually putting them on a patient and having them work in the mouth is a big jump. We're dealing with the human body here, and how the teeth are going to respond to pressure is not 100 percent predictable on a very minute scale, so orthodontists can't be as precise as they would like to be. But if you go the traditional braces route, then you might want to find out if any orthodontist you're considering uses fully customizable braces, because they are more precise.

A step down from fully customizable, but still better for fitting traditional braces, is the "indirect bonding" method. I'll go into more detail about that method in chapter 4, "All Braces Are Not Equal," but it involves placing brackets on a custom model of the patient's teeth first and then transferring them to the patient's actual teeth, which allows the orthodontist to place them more accurately.

A Revolution for Your Benefit

Now imagine an ideal scenario, where we could design custom braces or clear aligners that had all of the final positions of the teeth designed into the appliance. You could wear the appliance and, over the months, the teeth would all move into their preset ideal positions—and then you'd be done. There wouldn't be any adjustment appointments along the way. You'd need little or no input from your doctor during the treatment, meaning very few appointments to see them. It would all be designed at the beginning and come out perfect in the end.

Well, folks, that's pretty much where we are now with Invisalign. In my practice, that's how we do it. Let me tell you about how Invisalign has revolutionized the way orthodontics works in my practice.

In the late 1990s, the Align Technology company invented "clear plastic aligners" to move teeth instead of using braces, which, in my opinion, may be the greatest advance in the history of orthodontic care. Invisalign clear aligners looked like very thin versions of the mouth guards athletes wore. However, the similarity ended with their appearance.

These aligners eliminated the bracket-wire friction problem entirely, allowing the teeth to be moved more comfortably, quickly, and easily. Using computer modeling, the aligners are produced in sets perfectly matched to the patient's teeth and to the pace with which the orthodontist wanted to move the patient's teeth. These *truly* customized aligners also eliminate the movement of teeth that don't need to be moved. This approach has made orthodontics quicker and less painful.

Invisalign clear aligners are a lot more comfortable than traditional braces. For one thing, you don't have a mouthful of metal brackets and wires. And because of the elasticity of the plastic material, there's a restriction on how much pressure you can put on the teeth. The material is stiff enough to move a tooth but flexible enough that it will stretch over a crooked tooth and then apply a little bit of force to move the tooth. Because there's a limit to the amount of pressure we can put on the teeth, treatment with clear aligners is not nearly as painful as treatment with traditional braces.

Invisalign has also made wearing braces more convenient. If you've had traditional braces yourself, or known anyone who has, you'll know about the severe pain, large number of appointments, food getting caught in them, brackets breaking, the tiny rubber bands getting lost, speech being adversely affected because of having a mouth full of metal, and, finally, the difficulty of flossing and brushing. That last one is particularly important, because increased cavities are one of the biggest problems with wearing braces—and trying to get patients to floss and brush is always a challenge, even in a situation like this, when it's so important.

Invisalign clear plastic aligners eliminate *all* of these problems. There are no metal wires or brackets to break, and no sharp wires to stab you in the cheeks or lips. The braces are so thin that they don't affect the positioning of the lips or the tongue, which are the two things we use to form words, so they barely affect talking. And if food gets caught in or behind the aligners, they can be easily removed and quickly rinsed and the teeth easily brushed and flossed—which also eliminates the cavity problem that is caused by food residue remaining lodged in traditional braces.

Then there is the question of appearance. Very few people, young or old, like the way they look with metal braces on their teeth. A lot of attempts have been made to decrease the prominence of traditional braces in the mouth. Companies have come up with white, or clear, ceramic brackets to match the teeth better—but there is still a gray wire all around the teeth that looks odd when people smile. Other companies have marketed wires painted white—but they are a stark white that still shows up oddly against the different colors of teeth. They've even come up with a clear version of the tiny rubber bands—but the problem with those is that they absorb colors from food, so in a few weeks, after you've eaten things like spaghetti sauce and ketchup, they turn orange!

You also don't need to visit the orthodontist nearly as often with Invisalign clear aligners. The adjusting that must be done to the wires to move teeth with traditional braces is eliminated—the adjustment of the teeth is programmed into each of the aligners. (We'll get into the details of how this is done in chapter 4, "All Braces Are Not Equal.") You have a numbered set of those aligners and a plan that tells you when to move on to the next aligner—which, over time, will move your teeth ever so gradually into their new, ideal position. So, you just take out the aligners you've been wearing, and put in the new aligners—no need to see an orthodontist to do that!

Don't Settle for Less

It's important for you to know that there are other companies that make clear aligners and most of them are inferior to Invisalign, in my opinion. Their aligners are thicker, they're bulkier, and they're stiffer, so they're not nearly as comfortable to wear and they affect the movement of the lips and tongue more, which negatively affects speech. They do not use the most important component of tooth movement with clear aligners, which are attachments. Attachments are small geometric bumps of tooth-colored composite that are bonded onto certain teeth to make them move. Without attachments, only minor tooth misalignment can be corrected. This is why you may hear from the doctor, "Your case is too difficult for clear aligners. You have to have braces." They are limited in the degree of difficulty they can treat. If you're going to go with clear aligners, why wouldn't you want to go with the best? So far, I have not encountered a case so difficult that I could not treat it with Invisalign to the same or better result that I would get with braces.

If you're going to go with clear aligners, why wouldn't you want to go with the best?

I have used Invisalign for 99 percent of my patients—and they're happy I do. I have no stake in the company that makes Invisalign; I just have my experience as an orthodontist, watching the Invisalign folks spend the time, money, and brainpower to develop an appliance, and a process for creating and using it, that is far superior to any other aligners and process I've encountered over the twenty-five years I've been in practice.

When you interview orthodontists about doing work on yourself or your child (and you should interview them—more on that in the next chapter), be sure to find out if they use Invisalign, and if so, how much—what is their level of expertise with this product that can make your treatment, or your child's treatment, so much faster and easier. Can they treat any level of difficulty with Invisalign?

At this point, you might well ask, "If Invisalign clear aligners are so *far* superior to traditional braces and other clear aligners, why don't all orthodontists use them?" The fact is, not all doctors are equally skilled, not all doctors are as up-to-date with the latest technologies and treatments, and not all doctors have your wants and needs in mind in the way I believe they should. I'll talk more about that in the next chapter, and give you a bit of advice on what to look for in an orthodontist.

KEEP THIS IN MIND

- It is now possible to have your teeth aligned more quickly, more comfortably, and more conveniently, and you deserve to be treated that way.

- Traditional braces were the best technology we had for a long time, but they require a lot of time, discomfort, and expense that is no longer necessary.

- Invisalign clear plastic aligners are a revolutionary approach to teeth straightening that gives the same results in the smallest amount of time with the least discomfort.

CHAPTER TWO

All Doctors Are Not Equal

I f you're like most people, when you walk into a doctor's office one of the last things you check out is the diploma on the wall. I find this a bit odd since you're putting your body in the hands of a stranger, so it should be natural to want to confirm that this stranger is qualified to do what he or she is going to do. I guess this is because patients assume all doctors are the same. But there's something you need to keep in mind about that diploma. Every doctor has one. The person who had straight As gets a degree of doctor, and so does the one who just barely squeaked by. Even if they graduated last in their class, they got a diploma— and it looks the same as the one that the top person in the class got.

By which I mean to say, orthodontic doctors are like all human beings: some are hardworking, some are not; some keep up with the latest technology and practices, others do pretty much the same thing their whole career; some put you, the patient,

> *The person who had straight As gets a degree of doctor, and so does the one who just barely squeaked by.*

first, others put themselves and their prosperity first. And the diploma won't tell you any of that. You need to know what orthodontics is about, so you can talk to any orthodontist you consider using and figure out what kind of practice they run. That's one of the purposes of this book, to educate you, so you know what to ask about.

General and Pediatric Dentists Are Not Orthodontic Specialists

The thing that surprises me the most when people interview me about doing orthodontic work is that they don't even understand the distinction between what I do and what their family dentist does. It surprises me because I had to work so hard to become an orthodontist and all I do, day in and day out, is orthodontics—which is very different from restoring cavities, making crowns, developing overall oral health, and so on, which is what a family or pediatric dentist does.

An orthodontist must go through two to three years of additional special training *after* becoming a dentist to learn how to do orthodontics, just as in medicine a cardiologist must have additional training to learn how to do work on the heart, or a dermatologist on the skin, and so on. That additional training qualifies me to do things with the teeth and jaws that a non-orthodontist does not know how to do.

Now, in both dentistry and medicine, any doctor is legally *allowed* to do any type of procedure. For example, a family medicine physician can legally do heart surgery—and they do know something about the heart. But, of course, people want to put their lives in the hands of a specialist to lower the risk of an unsuccessful procedure. If they do need heart surgery, they go to a heart surgeon who does that procedure day in and day out, and has become really good at it. Your teeth may not be as important as your heart, but they *are* important to how you look and to your overall health. If your teeth need straightening or your palate needs to be expanded, why would you want someone less than an expert, who does these procedures daily, to perform them?

All of which is to say, it's a big mistake to lump dentists and orthodontists together—so beware of any dentist who claims to be able to do procedures normally done by orthodontists. Most dentists just don't have the training or experience to do those procedures as well as an orthodontist. There are plenty of examples of people getting hurt when things are not done correctly—in medicine and orthodontics. There are no "bargains" when it comes to complex orthodontic procedures.

This is not to say that there are *no* doctors that are not specialists in a particular field who are capable of doing some of these procedures. Some of them truly are capable. They may have a special passion for a particular area of dentistry or medicine and so they study it and know it really well. The problem is, it is difficult for you to determine who they are. Just because family dentists claim to know how to fix your crooked teeth with Invisalign does not mean they are truly capable.

Unfortunately, because Invisalign *appears* easier to use than traditional braces (you'll see how complex the procedure really is for orthodontists in chapter 4), there are large dental companies that are forcing family dentists who work for them to do Invisalign work with patients, whether they want to or not. I have heard that some of these companies actually give the dentists a quota of two patients per month. This is scary to me—as a doctor *and* as a prospective patient.

When you are seeking orthodontic treatment for you or your family, it's a good bet that an orthodontist will know more than a typical family dentist. But not always. If your family dentist tells you he/she can fix your crooked teeth, you would be wise to get references from other patients and ask how many patients the doctor has treated. Try to get as much information as you can about their experience level. If they answer your questions to your satisfaction (and you'll know a lot more about what to ask about after reading this book), then go ahead and have them do the treatment.

Choose Your Orthodontist Wisely

However, even if you go with an orthodontist, remember what I said about not all doctors being equal—the diploma on the wall notwithstanding. Do your research: get opinions and talk to the orthodontists you're considering—using what you learn from this book to hone your questions. If you go into an interview with an orthodontist knowing what kind of treatment and service you want, then you'll be much better able to determine if this particular doctor can do what you want done the way you want it done.

> *Do your research: get opinions and talk to the orthodontists you're considering.*

When you do your research, check out patient reviews. These are patients expressing their personal opinions—there's no objective ranking or classification of the skill level of the doctor. Getting opinions from other patients is a great way to see how the doctor has treated other patients and whether they were happy with the results. That at least tells you something about how the doctor treats patients, and I think it is important. Get referrals from your friends and neighbors. Talk to them about the office. This is probably the best way to get the scoop on a doctor's office.

When you interview an orthodontist, you want to find out why you should choose them, what makes them better than the orthodontist down the street, how well they stay abreast of the latest technologies and techniques in orthodontics by doing training and continuing education, what kind of braces and other appliances and techniques they're expert with, and how long they expect the treatment to take—and, of course, the cost of that treatment. I think it is also important to ask what protocols they have in place to decrease the amount of treatment a patient needs.

Unfortunately, I know doctors who take a lot of continuing education, but I wouldn't go to them or send my family to them, because even though they're really smart, and they know a lot about what's going on with technology, they're kind of unscrupulous people, doing a lot of treatments that are unnecessary and superexpensive for their patients. Which means you need to ask doctors about their ethics, their morality almost.

I would ask, "What are your thoughts on being as conservative as possible with my treatment, about getting the best outcome without having to do a lot of complicated things? What could we do to solve my problem using the most conservative, simplest approach to get us the best end result for the least amount of money? What would that option look like?" I guarantee you that not many doctors have been asked this kind of question, so you'll catch them off guard and ought to get a response that's revealing and genuine.

You should also ask them how they take the jaw (TMJ) and the bite into account when they're straightening teeth. It's surprising how many orthodontists don't do this, because balancing those things is difficult. It can cause a lot of pain and suffering for people if their bite isn't correct. It can cause them to wear teeth down, or crack or break teeth, and a lot of times you then lose the teeth because they're not fixable anymore, so they have to be pulled. It can also lead to jaw problems such as TMD (also known as TMJ). Taking the jaw and bite into consideration is essential, so make sure any orthodontist you consider will do that. Did they even look at your TMJ when they did the examination? Did they ask if you had ever had any problems with it?

WHAT TO ASK ANY ORTHODONTIST YOU CONSIDER

- "Why do you recommend that I choose you as my orthodontist? What makes you better than the orthodontist down the street?"

- "How do you stay abreast of the latest and greatest technologies and techniques in orthodontics?"

- "What kinds of braces and other appliances do you use? Do you use Invisalign? If so, how extensively? Do you consider yourself an Invisalign expert? Why or why not? Can you treat difficult cases with Invisalign as successfully as you can with braces?"

- "How do you take the jaw and the bite into account when you're straightening teeth? Do you have special training in the area of the jaw joint and the bite?"

- "How long do you expect my treatment to take and what do you expect it to cost?"

- "What are your thoughts on being as conservative as possible with treatments, about getting the best outcome without having to do a lot of complicated treatment? What could we do to solve my problem using the most conservative, simplest approach to get us the best end result for the least amount of money and time? What would that option look like?"

In my current practice, I'm able to treat orthodontic problems at a much more complex level—both because of my two-and-a-half decades of experience in orthodontics and because of my high level of expertise with Invisalign. When I treat patients this way, I make sure we deal with any problems associated with the jaw or the bite in conjunction with getting their teeth straightened—the balanced approach I mentioned in the previous paragraph. In my opinion, you can't just straighten someone's teeth without taking the jaw and bite into account.

Getting back to choosing an orthodontist, one of the reasons it's important to find one who is well informed and honest is because there are far too many orthodontists out there who are willing to do unnecessary procedures just because it's profitable for them. Or maybe they half believe the procedures will do something, but they've never really looked into the research that shows these procedures have no effect that couldn't have been achieved later. One of my pet peeves is orthodontists who perform unnecessary procedures on little children, and I'll take that up in the next chapter.

KEEP THIS IN MIND

- An orthodontic residency diploma tells you nothing about how skilled and dedicated an orthodontist is—the graduate who squeaks by receives the same diploma the one hard-working doctor who graduated at the top of the class.

- You need to interview any orthodontist you're considering to do work on yourself or your child, using the information you're learning in this book and the specific questions in this chapter.

- Straightening teeth is just one aspect of orthodontic health; it needs to be balanced with consideration of the jaw (TMJ) and bite.

CHAPTER THREE

The Earlier, the Better Is Not Always True

One day a mother brought her little boy in to see me. He was eight or nine years old and had a very severe underbite. I told the mom that I did not recommend doing any orthodontic treatment on him because his bite was so severe that he was absolutely going to have to have jaw surgery eventually. There was really no way around it. Of course, no parent wants to hear that, so she went down the street to an orthodontist who's more than happy to do early treatment on any kid who comes in the door. He told her, "You know, this is a great time for us to get in there and try to change what's happening with his facial skeleton, because he's growing so much. We can take advantage of his growth, and try to avoid him having surgery later." She loved this, of course, so she went with this orthodontist's plan.

Four years later, this same mother showed up in my office with her second son. I didn't recognize her, of course, because I'd only met her once and she had never come back. Her second son had exactly the same problem as the first one, so I told her the same story that

I'd told her before, with the first kid. Then she said, "You probably don't remember me, but I came to see you about four years ago with my older son. You told me exactly the same thing, but I didn't want to listen to you. So, I took him someplace else and I got treatment for him."

Of course, in my mind, I was thinking she's going to say, "And the treatment worked great and you're an idiot." So, I sat there, sweating, and she said, "You know what? You were so right, and that's why I'm back in your office. The other orthodontist told me he could change the facial growth. We worked with him for three years and we did everything he told us to do. My son wore headgear and expanders and braces. And after those three years were over, he looked worse than he did before he started!"

So, I asked her how the orthodontist explained this lack of results.

"Well, I said to him, 'What's going on here? You told me you could fix him because he was growing so much.' And he said, 'Well, you know what? He's just *growing so much*. He's growing in an unfavorable way. There's just nothing I can do about that.' And he basically kicked us out of his office."

I looked her in the eye and said, "I feel horrible that that happened to you—I really do—but I have to say, I told you so." We had a chuckle over that.

There was just no way that her son was fixable without surgery. Yet she had paid this other orthodontist $4,000 to $5,000—and now he was telling her exactly what I told her four years before. Now, she has to spend $20,000 to get jaw surgery for her son, and then another $5,000 or $6,000 for braces. She wasted $5,000 on a first set of braces that her son should have never have had in the first place!

Myths about Early Orthodontics

There's a school of thought in orthodontics today about treating young kids, called "dento-facial orthopedics." Many times, we recommend starting treatment on kids as early as five years old. At that stage of the game, they only have their baby teeth, which are not permanent. (The technical term for baby teeth in dentistry is "primary teeth.")

"Dento-facial orthopedics" refers to moving around the facial bones, guiding dento-facial growth by doing appliance therapy. Your orthodontist is telling you that your child has dental problems and that, if you start early, they can be more easily corrected. Or maybe they say the child has an underlying skeletal discrepancy, and they can change facial growth. But the number-one problem they talk about is there not being enough room for all the permanent teeth. Because there's not adequate room for the permanent teeth, they say, you need to start doing some appliance therapy to start growing the mouth, making it bigger. This is called "arch development."

THE TRUTH ABOUT CHILDREN'S DENTAL DEVELOPMENT

Six, seven, or eight is the typical age when the lower and the upper permanent teeth start coming in. Because of this, the American Association of Orthodontics (AAO) recommends that kids that age should be going to the orthodontist for their first evaluation. I definitely agree that children should be coming in around age seven, so they can be screened, and we can start looking at what's going to be happening with their teeth over the next few years.

One of the great things orthodontists can do at this point is catch developing tooth-eruption problems early on. Then they can guide the eruption of permanent teeth effectively, without trauma and inexpensively, by judiciously extracting a baby/primary tooth here or there—avoiding orthodontic treatment altogether at this young age. Removing a tooth makes it easier for the permanent tooth to erupt into the empty space where the baby tooth once was, so the doctor can guide an erupting permanent tooth into the mouth along this easier path. This allows the permanent teeth to come in along the path of least resistance. And if the tooth doesn't come in correctly, *then* you can consider actual orthodontic treatment. I believe in being conservative, helping the body do what it can do on its own, first, before resorting to expensive, painful, high-maintenance orthodontic treatment.

> *I believe in being conservative, helping the body do what it can do on its own, first, before resorting to expensive, painful, high-maintenance orthodontic treatment.*

Using this method, we can avoid having to do orthodontic treatment on little children—trying to widen the palate and that kind of thing—saving the family thousands of dollars plus all of the hassles of the appointments, and nagging the child about brushing, and all the stuff that goes on during orthodontic treatment for young patients. Some orthodontists will try to guilt parents into getting treatment—and nobody wants to feel like a bad parent, right?—but it really isn't necessary most of the time.

There are a few other situations where early orthodontic treatment is actually necessary, and those have to do with the upper jawbone, palate, or maxilla being too narrow, so that, when the patient bites down, the back teeth fit inside the bite with the lower teeth. That can happen on one side of the mouth or on both sides, depending on the severity of the constriction of the palate. These are called "skeletal crossbites."

Correcting a skeletal crossbite is a legitimate reason for doing palate expansion on a younger child. But the term "younger child' is relative. Orthodontists can predictably expand the palate up through twelve years of age—and some studies say up through fifteen years. With skeletal crossbites there is a side-to-side shifting of the bite in some children to try and get the teeth to fit together better. This is called a "functional shift." This may cause problems to the developing jaw joint (TMJ) and the muscles of the jaws. These are called TMJ problems or TMD. Doing palatal expansion on younger children is a good idea in these cases. I treat a lot of patients with TMJ problems, so I've seen that it can be beneficial to correct functional shifts and skeletal crossbites early.

Sometimes, one or more upper front teeth erupt behind some of the lower front teeth. This is called a "dental crossbite." It is different than a skeletal crossbite because it is caused by some teeth erupting into the incorrect position, not by an underlying jaw bone discrepancy. These are also good to correct early, as there is a very high chance of some of these teeth being cracked or broken due to how they fit in the bite.

THE TRUTH ABOUT THE LIMITS OF EARLY ORTHODONTICS

Another event that often motivates parents to look into orthodontic work is when their children's adult (permanent) teeth begin to come in. Those teeth are twice as big as the baby teeth, so parents start panicking about how all those big teeth are going to fit in that little mouth.

They'll also say, "If we do this phase-one treatment (a.k.a. early treatment), then we may not have to do the second phase of treatment," or, "If we do have to have a second phase of treatment, it will be shorter, easier, and cheaper." That sure does sound good when you're a parent deciding about putting out the money for phase one. If you see the potential for saving some money and hassle later, then you're much more likely to go forward with the early treatment. The problem is, I don't see that actually happen—except in rare cases.

What these orthodontists don't explain to the parents is that the teeth looking too big is *normal* at this stage of development, that "phase one" isn't necessary most of the time. They don't explain that later on, as their kid starts losing back molar teeth, they're actually going to gain space. When they're eleven, twelve, and thirteen years old, when they're getting in the rest of their permanent teeth, their bodies have grown significantly. Things change a lot between seven years of age and thirteen years of age. You need to allow time for kids to mature and grow into their permanent, *adult* teeth. You don't need to interfere with the natural human dental growth pattern except in rare cases.

It's amazing how often kids just grow out of the majority of dental problems—things typically get better, not worse. The cases where things get worse are only when we have these very unusually large skeletal discrepancies, such as a severe underbite. They have a small upper jaw and a big lower jaw, or vice versa. Those are things we can't fix orthodontically; they have to be surgically corrected when kids are done growing, in their early to midtwenties.

You may be wondering why am I going against the grain of most of the orthodontic profession. It is because I rarely do early treatment, I do not extract permanent teeth on very many patients, and I do jaw surgery only when absolutely required—and yet my patients' teeth get fixed. I know that avoiding early treatment works.

THE TRUTH ABOUT ORTHODONTICS AND SLEEP APNEA/SNORING

"Obstructive sleep apnea" is a medical disorder where a person's airway is blocked during sleeping. Basically, they are suffocating while they sleep. This disorder can affect patients at any age, even children and infants. There are oral appliances for treating sleep apnea that hold the lower jaw in a forward position to help keep the airway open, and they work pretty well. I do that kind of treatment in my practice. They don't work as well as a CPAP, the little ventilator machine, but some people just can't tolerate those, so these oral appliances are a great secondary option. Dentists and orthodontists have now discovered that the "arch development" they do on little kids may also be a great way to treat sleep apnea. This treatment can be done on adults as well and is a really promising new treatment approach.

There's actually a national company trying to franchise early orthodontic treatment on children that have sleep apnea. They use expanders and mandible-advancing appliances under the theory that the mouth will be bigger and there will be room for the tongue to come forward, so it doesn't go back in the throat and block the airway. The roof of the mouth is also the floor of the nose, and this procedure also expands the nasal airway, so that kids can breathe better through their nose.

Now, this is a great treatment. Because it's a medical problem, no dentist or orthodontist can legally diagnose sleep apnea, but they can help treat it. Most informed orthodontists screen for "obstructive sleep apnea" (OSA) in their patients. If they suspect that a patient has this disorder, then they should be referred to a sleep specialist for further evaluation.

In children especially, large tonsils can also block the airway and simply removing them can correct the problem. This is something that must be evaluated by the orthodontist, and a proper referral to an ear, nose, and throat (ENT) specialist should be done if large tonsils are found.

OTHER REASONS FOR EARLY TREATMENT

Both of *my* children had early treatment. They both had situations that required it, so I'll describe those additional examples (along with crossbite problems) of when you might want early treatment.

My son developed a serious infection in the gums around his lower front teeth. His teeth were really crowded and, believe it or not, he got a piece of corn on the cob stuck down under his gums. It took us a while to finally get it out, and his gums would just never heal up after that. I had to put braces on those teeth to straighten them out, just so we could clean his teeth more easily. Then the infection went away.

There are situations like that, where you have teeth so misaligned that it's actually causing an illness in the teeth or the gums. That's a legitimate reason to do early orthodontics.

My daughter falls into another category. Sometimes you have kids whose teeth come in and they look odd, they call attention to themselves. Now, we all know that kids—and even adults—can be cruel sometimes, so this situation can lead to significant self-esteem issues. All of a sudden, your child is getting teased at school every day about having crazy-looking teeth.

That's what happened to my daughter. Her front teeth protruded a bit and, because she was a state champion gymnast, that look was starting to bug her. Now she's getting treatment for that, and she feels better about herself. There's nothing wrong with that—as long as a child's parents understand that this is cosmetic, not something that's functionally necessary for the later development of the child's teeth. I am also expanding her palate because she has airway problems that are affecting her sleep.

Those are a couple of the other reasons that might lead parents to consider early orthodontic treatment.

If the parents and child are not bothered by small or large abnormalities with a child's developing teeth, and there are no functional problems potentially causing permanent damage, then they shouldn't be putting out a lot of money to fix those primary teeth, which are going to fall out within a few years, anyway. I don't think it's right for an orthodontist to pressure parents into having this kind of work done on a child—or, worse yet, to make the child feel self-conscious, as if this work is absolutely necessary.

Make an Informed Decision

Keep in mind, though, that, for the majority of children, this early work is simply not necessary. My own practice is close to 50 percent adults, and a lot of these adult patients never had orthodontic treatment when they were little—or even as teenagers—and yet I'm still able to fix their orthodontic problems without much hassle. Orthodontists are telling people that they need to have their children's teeth problems fixed when the kids are eight or nine years old, or they'll need jaw surgery later. This is one of the biggest scare tactics orthodontists use, and unfortunately it often works. One orthodontist even told a couple who later came to me that it was "borderline child abuse" if they didn't get a procedure like this done. But I'm fixing most of these problems on adults all the time, with orthodontics, not jaw surgery.

Don't just accept these scare tactics. Look the orthodontist in the eye and ask, "If I don't have this treatment done for my child now, what is going to be the worst possible thing that could happen?" Look into it, ask other orthodontists, look online, and make sure it's really necessary to have the work done in childhood. More often than not, you'll find out that it isn't necessary.

I often have people come to me for a second opinion about a treatment that's been recommended for their child, and the conversation often goes like this:

Parents: "We were told that there's going to be a big problem later if we don't get this fixed right way."

Me: "What did they tell you the big problem was going to be?"

No answer for a moment, and they have that deer-in-the-headlights look in their eyes.

Parents: "Well, they never said exactly what the problem was going to be; they just said it was a big problem."

Me: "So they said it was going to be a big problem, but they didn't tell you what the big problem was going to be; is that accurate?"

Parents: "Yes."

Me: "Okay. Would you like me to tell you what the big problem is going to be?"

Parents: "Of course."

Me: "The big problem is going to be that they won't make the payment on their car or boat."

They always laugh at this. But the weird thing is—and this is one of the reasons I'm writing the book—I have to work harder to educate people why treatment may not be necessary people than I have to work convincing them that they *do* need treatment.

You also need to keep in mind that every type of dental treatment also has its downside. There is the potential for iatrogenic damage to the teeth, or the gums, or the TMJ. In many cases, like all medical treatment, the best orthodontic treatment that you can get is no treatment at all, because of those inherent risks. You're better off not taking on those risks unless your child really needs the treatment, or you really want it and understand what it involves.

The risks and rewards of orthodontic work—at any age—have something to do with what kind of appliance the orthodontist uses. In the next chapter, I'll educate you about the choice of braces available, so when you make that choice, you'll know what you're getting into.

KEEP THIS IN MIND

- Most young children do not need orthodontic work when they still have half their baby teeth and half their permanent teeth—and that work will not necessarily decrease the need for orthodontic work when their permanent teeth are completely in.

- Judiciously extracting primary teeth is usually enough to make room in a child's mouth for "crowded" or misplaced teeth to come in correctly.

- Dentists and orthodontists are not legally allowed to diagnose sleep apnea, so don't have work done on your child's mouth to treat sleep apnea without a medical diagnosis that your child has this condition unless there are other concurrent dental problems you are correcting at the same time. That way, you get the dental problem corrected and perhaps correct the breathing and sleeping issue at the same time.

CHAPTER FOUR

All Braces Are Not Equal

As I mentioned earlier, braces have come a long way over the last couple decades, although plenty of people still use the old-fashioned kind—and you'll be given that choice when you see an orthodontist, so you need to know about all of your choices, so you know what to ask about them.

Today, there are essentially two kinds of braces, the traditional kind with brackets and metal wires, which have a few variations that I'll get into, and clear aligners, which differ from each other in their level of precision, predictability, and sophistication.

By the time you finish this chapter, you'll know exactly what will go on, inside and outside of your mouth, when you choose one kind of braces or the other. You'll also understand that there are varying levels of sophistication in how orthodontists work with braces, which

By the time you finish this chapter, you'll know exactly what will go on, inside and outside of your mouth, when you choose one kind of braces or the other.

will help you keep an eye out for an orthodontist who knows enough to make your experience of having braces as short and, if not exactly pleasant—we can't work miracles—as pleasant as possible.

Traditional Twin-Bracket Braces

The classic braces are called "twin brackets," because the rectangular brackets that are affixed to the teeth for the wire to go through have two (twin) little protrusions on them that we call "wings." A narrow slot runs horizontally through both wings and the wire fits into that slot. The wire that connects all of the brackets together is called an "arch wire." The wings also have hooks on the top and bottom, and little colored rubber bands are engaged on those hooks to hold the wire in the brackets.

The way that the slots and the wire interact is the important part of how orthodontists move teeth. The slot is a precisely sized and shaped rectangular slot. The wires are also precisely sized and shaped, so when we first start off doing orthodontic treatment and the teeth are crooked, we have to put the brackets on each tooth in the best position to move that particular tooth, over time, into its ideal final position.

The brackets are bonded onto the surface of the teeth with an amazing composite glue that is both incredibly strong and still able to be easily removed when the braces are no longer needed. Placing those brackets correctly is the great art of orthodontic work. The orthodontist must understand exactly where to place the bracket on each tooth so that it moves the tooth in the right direction and distance. Then we thread this really small wire through all the bracket slots on the crooked teeth—and the straight ones, too, of course, because all of the teeth have to move together. These days, the wire we use is made out of a special kind of material called nickel titanium, which is a metal that you can deform but doesn't take a permanent bend. It will always go back to its original horseshoe or dental arch shape. This creates pressure on the teeth, which moves them gradually into new positions.

As the teeth get straighter and we want to have more and more control over the exact positioning of the teeth, we go from the classic wire—which if you look at it in cross section is round like most wires are—to square, and then, ultimately, to a rectangular shape that very closely approximates the shape and size of the slot in the bracket. The sizes of the wires also increase as the cross-sectional shape changes.

The wire is what allows us to move teeth. The brackets are how we attach the wire to the teeth. When you go to the orthodontist to have your braces adjusted, that's what he's adjusting, the wire. He's putting in different sizes of wire and wires that are made out of different kinds of materials. The first wire, the round one, fits more loosely, so the torque (control of the tooth roots) isn't as precise. We use that wire for getting the gross alignment of the teeth. Then the next size wire is most often a rectangular wire, which fits into that rectangular-shaped slot a little bit more tightly, so now we can start getting more control over the positions of the root of the teeth, because in order to align the crown of the tooth, we also have to align the roots.

But you can't put too much force on the roots, because you can damage them, so the orthodontist must judge when the teeth are ready to take the torque of the square wire over the round wire. The more tightly we can grab hold of the tooth, the more precise the movement we can achieve. As we go from a round shape and progress through to the square and then rectangular shapes, we're getting more and more detailed control over the positioning of the tooth.

Then, ultimately, we put in a wire that's made out of stainless steel. Unlike the previous nickel titanium wires, this wire is actually bendable—it doesn't spring back like the nickel-titanium wires—so the orthodontist can use small pliers to put specific bends in the wires to move specific teeth into their perfect final position. You can only make very small bends at one time, so you have to progressively, over the course of several appointments, make the bends bigger and bigger to finally move the tooth where you want it to be.

It's because of this last part of the process that orthodontists are sometimes called "wire benders." It takes a lot of knowledge, care, and precision to bend those wires in exactly the right way that will make each tooth, including its root, move into its proper position.

That's why orthodontics is a specialty, because it's very complicated to do this in a precise way, so that you end up with a good result as quickly as possible, but also do it in a safe way, so that you're not causing problems. Some people seem to look at braces as if they were a toy, but, in fact, they're a dangerous weapon that can cause serious damage to teeth if they're not used correctly. Orthodontics is sometimes oversimplified by the public, and even by some general dentists, because everybody thinks it's just a simple thing: you put the braces on the teeth and the teeth magically move where they're supposed to go. But that could not be further from the truth. This also relates back to chapter 2, "All Doctors Are Not Equal," because not all orthodontists are equally skilled at this kind of thoughtful, precise work, so you need to vet them.

THE DISADVANTAGES OF TWIN-BRACKET BRACES

Clinically, there are really two big downsides to twin-bracket braces. Number one is getting cavities on your teeth. Having all of that hardware in your mouth for two to five years makes it much harder to floss and brush your teeth, which can cause a lot of cavities. There was actually a court case where an orthodontist got sued for leaving the braces on a patient who wasn't keeping his teeth clean. The child ended up with $10,000 or $15,000 worth of damage to his teeth when his braces came off. Now, in most practices, if patients are not keeping their teeth clean, treatment must be stopped and the braces removed.

The other clinical downside is that traditional braces can cause the roots of the teeth to actually get shorter. This is called "root resorption." There's been a lot of research done into what causes root resorption, and there's not a clear answer yet, but there seems to be a connection with placing heavy forces on the teeth, the way braces do. Also, longer treatment also seems to have an effect.

The practical disadvantages of traditional braces are well known to anyone who's ever worn them or had a child who wore them. For one thing, they're often extremely uncomfortable, especially during the first week after they've been adjusted by the orthodontist. You also have to be very careful with what you eat, because any kind of hard food—pizza crust, nuts, chips, hard candy, etc.—can break the arch wire or the brackets, which not only hurts but also requires a trip to the orthodontist's office for repair. Food can get caught in the braces and be difficult to dislodge. The brackets can cut into the cheeks, if the face is struck or strikes anything (such as when a patient falls on their face playing soccer). So, living with traditional braces is a constant challenge.

The final disadvantage of traditional braces is how visible they are. There's been lots of humor in movies and TV shows around how unattractive traditional braces look, and, of course, this is one of the reasons people resist getting them. Orthodontic device companies are always trying to find something to make the hardware less visible, but their solutions are not great.

Years ago, they invented brackets that are made out of ceramic porcelain. Some of them are clear and look like they're made out of glass, so they're not so visible. But those brackets are a nightmare to work with, because they're brittle and they break constantly. They're also uncomfortable because they have sharp edges. Every time one of them breaks, the patient must come in and get them replaced. It's a hassle for the patient. The brackets can also shatter when the orthodontist tries to do certain tooth movements, so the treatment takes longer.

When it comes to appearance—which is the whole point of clear brackets—you still have the wire threaded through the brackets. So, you might have brackets that aren't that obvious, but you still have a gray line across your teeth. Some companies have come up with a coating they put on the wire that makes them white, but it's *really* white, so, now, instead of a gray line on your teeth, you have a visible white line on your teeth that doesn't match your teeth color. Companies have also made totally clear rubber bands to hold the wire in the clear braces, but they absorb food colors like crazy, so within a few days they aren't clear any more.

Self-Ligating Braces

Self-ligating braces are just a small variation on traditional twin-bracket braces, but some orthodontists sell them hard to their patients as a great advance in orthodontics—which I don't agree with, but you need to know what they are, in case an orthodontist offers them to you. The main difference with self-ligating braces is that instead of having the little rubber bands that hold the wire into the slot, there's a little sliding cover on the bracket that goes over the wire and holds it in place.

The benefit of this, supposedly, is that there's less friction between the arch wire and the bracket slot, which allows the orthodontist to apply a lower force to the teeth, so the teeth don't hurt as much. Putting less force on the teeth should also help decrease the chance of root resorption, the shortening of the teeth's roots discussed earlier. Finally, the teeth should move more quickly.

That's the big sales pitch for self-ligating brackets, that they're lower friction and the teeth move less painfully than they do when using rubber bands. They're also supposed to make the treatment go faster. But, in my opinion, this is mostly marketing hoopla. There may be a *little bit* less friction, but the companies that make self-ligating brackets have never been able to prove in any sort of meaningful way that there is actually significantly less friction clinically. Those tiny rubber bands on regular braces just don't cause that much friction. In my opinion, it's really a marketing ploy to sell a bracket that costs significantly more than a traditional twin bracket.

The only reason I ever used self-ligating braces was because the company that first produced them also came up with a fully customizable, digital system for placing brackets on the teeth—and that was a real advance in orthodontics, so I worked with their braces and their system for a while. Which is a good segue to the subject of fully customized metal braces.

Fully Customized Metal Braces

Fully customized metal braces come in two varieties. One has only customized digital wires for any type of braces and the other has custom wires and brackets. The principle is where images of the existing teeth are fed into a computer, and then a plan is developed for how to move the teeth from where they are to their ideal positions.

Fully customized metal braces still need to rely on wires and brackets, so what is produced are sets of computer-positioned brackets and custom wires that are threaded through those brackets on a scheduled plan. The custom wires are bent by computer-controlled robots according to the plan for the movement of each tooth—a task that the orthodontist usually performs by hand. This approach increases the level of precision when placing the brackets and when creating the bends in the wires that move the teeth, because it's all computer-assisted. This higher precision allows us to not have to adjust the braces as often and to move the teeth to their ideal positions in a shorter period of time.

Another type of custom braces that is not digital is called "indirect bonding." This consists of making a model of a patient's teeth, and then bonding the braces onto that plaster model. Once the brackets are placed as ideally as possible on the plaster teeth, we make a clear plastic cover that fits over the brackets—it looks kind of like a mouth guard. Then we pull the brackets off of the model of the teeth and the brackets are embedded into this cover. Finally, we use the cover with the brackets embedded into it to actually transfer the brackets to the patient's teeth, so the brackets end up on the patient's teeth exactly where we put them on the model. (The advantage to this is that we don't have a tongue and cheeks obstructing our view of the teeth as we try to place the brackets on them).

Clear Aligners

As I noted earlier, clear aligners were invented by Invisalign and they have changed the way orthodontics can be done. I also noted that other companies make clear aligners, but, in my opinion, none of them approach the sophistication of Invisalign's materials, designs, and processes. For that reason, I'm going to focus on working with Invisalign clear aligners in this description.

Other companies make clear aligners, but, in my opinion, none of them approach the sophistication of Invisalign's materials, designs, and processes.

Invisalign clear aligners are made of a sophisticated clear plastic material that the company has continued to improve over the years. It is thin, flexible, and produces optimum force for moving teeth while remaining comfortable in the patient's mouth. There are also the ever-important attachments that are placed on the teeth to provide the precision and predictability we need to be able to treat any type of complex case. Attachments are small pieces of composite material in different geometric shapes and sizes—there are several different shapes: mainly squares and rectangles—that are bonded to the teeth. Without the attachments, only very simple and minor tooth movements can be done.

When a patient decides to use Invisalign braces, we first use an intraoral camera, called a "scanner," that takes 6,000 images *per second* to photograph the patient's teeth in minute detail. We send these images to Invisalign, which creates a computer model of the patient's teeth.

When we get the model, we sit down at the computer, to plan the teeth movements, and calculate where each of the attachments will go on the teeth to help achieve the desired teeth movement. Placing these attachments is best compared to placing the brackets on the teeth for traditional braces. Their location helps to direct the force of the clear aligners in the ideal direction for the tooth that needs to be moved. If a tooth is already in its ideal position, it needs no attachment (not all teeth that are moved need an attachment, either—it depends on the kind of movement necessary).

Once the attachment positions are determined, Invisalign uses its proprietary algorithms to produce as many sets of clear aligners, top and bottom, as are necessary to achieve the tooth movement plan over time. Each set is numbered in order, and the orthodontist tells the patient how long to wear each set before moving onto the next one. With this approach, there is no need to visit the orthodontist's office to make adjustments. The adjustments are built into the sequenced sets of aligners.

THE ADVANTAGES OF CLEAR ALIGNERS

If you're looking for a section on clear aligners that parallels "The Disadvantages of Twin-Bracket Braces," I'm afraid I have to disappoint you. Not only do clear aligners—at least, Invisalign clear aligners—*eliminate* all of the disadvantages of traditional braces that I outlined above, but they also don't *add* any disadvantages of their own. You can eat whatever you want, whenever you want. You won't have the cavity problem, because you're not likely to get food caught under them, because they hug your teeth tightly. But even if you do get food under them, you can take them out and rinse them in a minute.

Funny story. I had this Invisalign patient, Susie. Susie got her first set of Invisalign clear aligners and went home happy, but the next day she came marching back into my office and announced, "I want out of this Invisalign thing, right now, and I want you to switch me over to metal braces." I asked Susie why on earth she would want to do that. She said, "Because I went home with these aligners, and I showed them to my husband, and he said, 'What are you gonna do this summer when we're camping, and you gotta take these things out to eat and drink? You're gonna be losing them all the time!'"

I said, "Susie, when you're camping, I don't want you to take your aligners out ever, except when you brush your teeth. I want you to eat with them on. I want you to drink with them in. And then, when you get done eating, and you're on the river and you're drinking a beer, you can just quickly, when no one's looking, pull out your aligners, take a swig of beer, rinse it around in your mouth, and then spit it out on your aligners to get any food out of them. And then pop them back in your mouth and you're good to go."

We both laughed and she said, "I think I can do that!"

I don't think any story captures better how convenient clear aligners are. That was also when I realized that the aligners *would actually work faster if people ate with them on,* because when you eat with your aligners on, you're actually pushing the aligners onto your teeth with more force, which helps them move the teeth. One company actually sells these "chew toys" for people with clear aligners for exactly that purpose. But you don't need to buy something special to accomplish this; you just need to eat with them on. Bring on the steak and potatoes.

I now tell all of my patients to eat with their aligners on, and for many of them, it's cut *in half* the amount of time they need to wear any given set of aligners. Parents love this, too, of course, because they don't have to monitor their kids taking the aligners in and out (and, of course, at school they can't monitor them, anyway), so the aligners are much less likely to get lost.

The most important advantage of Invisalign clear aligners is how much faster they work at moving teeth.

The most important advantage of Invisalign clear aligners is how much faster they work at moving teeth. I'll get into the details of why this is true in the next chapter, "How to Have the Best Orthodontic Experience," but I want to note here that, by using Invisalign in my practice, we're *dramatically* cutting down the time that patients need to be in treatment. And my patients are more comfortable while it's happening.

The other obvious advantage of clear aligners is their visual subtlety. Compared to any kind of traditional metal braces, these thin, clear, plastic aligners, which hug your teeth, are a much-less-obtrusive presence.

Can you tell I'm a fan of Invisalign? If you have any doubt, the next chapter will put that to rest, as we explore how using the Invisalign approach will make your orthodontic experience so much quicker and more pleasant than you ever dreamed it could be.

KEEP THIS IN MIND

- There are essentially just two kinds of braces: traditional twin-bracket metal ones and clear plastic aligners.

- The disadvantages of traditional braces are well-known to most people: the wire and brackets break; they get food stuck in them, causing tooth decay; they're painful; they don't look good; the treatment can take three to five years.

- The advantages of clear aligners are less well known: there are no parts to break; food is less likely to get caught under them, and they can be rinsed immediately if it does; they're comfortable and not obtrusive visually; treatment can take as little as six months.

CHAPTER FIVE

How to Have the Best Orthodontic Experience

T he first step toward having the best orthodontic experience is to decide what your ultimate goal is, exactly what level of work you want done on your teeth or your kid's teeth, so the orthodontist understands what you want, and so you have clear expectations for the orthodontist you're choosing. It stands to reason that it's hard to choose the right orthodontist if you aren't clear about what kind of work you want an orthodontist to do. You have to communicate clearly with the doctor.

As doctors, we're trained to always give everyone the ideal, but, in the real world, a lot of people have things like crazy, messed up bites and they live perfectly fine with them. It doesn't affect the quality of their life or anything like that. Sometimes, I have conversations with my patients and I say that having things ideal is really awesome, but that there is also this thing in life called "good enough." Your teeth can go from being a long way away from the ideal to getting much closer to the ideal, but not actually achieving the ideal, and if the patient's comfortable with it, is healthy, and there are no functional problems, that's what we'll do. I say this because sometimes the amount of work and expense necessary to get ideal is not worth it. Many times, it involves jaw surgery with all of its inherent risks.

So, in short, your expectations about the results of your treatment need to be in line with what you ultimately want—do you want the ideal or are you okay with, "a lot better" is "good enough." Good enough is good enough for a lot of people.

Once you're clear about what you want, then you need to find a doctor who's competent to deliver the level of treatment you want. If you want to get an orthodontic treatment to help with your TMJ problem, then you'd better make sure that the orthodontist you choose is well versed in treating TMJ problems.

How do you find this out? In my office, I have patients who have agreed to speak with new patients about their experience having me treat their orthodontic problems, whatever those might have been. This is straight from the horse's mouth—so to speak. They're happy to explain to new patients what happens during the treatment and about what they liked and didn't like about it.

> *When you interview a prospective orthodontist, get references from their patients who've done the same treatment you're going to have.*

When you interview a prospective orthodontist, get references from their patients who've done the same treatment you're going to have. If the doctor is not willing to let you do that, then it would be a red flag to me. They might claim they can't do it because of patient confidentiality, but if they ask the patient and the patient agrees, that's not an issue. So don't take that excuse.

The Braces Make All the Difference

The next biggest choice you make, if you're getting braces—and most orthodontic work involves braces—is the kind of braces you choose. You read about the different types of braces in the last chapter, so you should be able to make an informed choice.

By now, I think I've made it clear that I believe choosing Invisalign clear aligners will go a long way toward making your orthodontic experience the best possible one. Metal braces have a raft of problems and don't move teeth as quickly and comfortably; ceramic alternatives are too fragile and will have you going back and forth to the doctor's office all the time for repairs; other clear aligners are clumsier and less efficient and may not be sophisticated enough to treat the complexity of your case. When it comes to the orthodontic experience, Invisalign is really the way to go.

If you can find an orthodontist who's savvy about using the Invisalign system, then you're going have the best possible orthodontic experience. It's going to go really quickly. It's not going to be appointment intensive. You're not going to have all those restrictions on your eating. The Invisalign system is simply

If you can find an orthodontist who's savvy about using the Invisalign system, then you're going have the best possible orthodontic experience.

head and shoulders above the conventional braces system. As far as I'm concerned, the choice is clear, which is why I use Invisalign with the vast majority of my orthodontic patients—and that includes the youngest ones.

So, just *how* quick and easy can treatment be with Invisalign? Let me tell you about how we do things in my office, because it points out very clearly the potential for an ideal orthodontic experience that the Invisalign system makes possible. Before I start in, however, I have to share a story about how we came up with the name for our approach.

It was "Bring Your Child to Work" day, I was in the car with my ten-year-old daughter, and we were on the way to my office.

"I've got a project for you to work on today," I said to her. "I need a new name for my approach to straightening teeth, and I'd like you to come up with it. The idea is that we work very quickly, and patients hardly ever have to come into the office, and we get great results. You've got all day to think about it, but, by the end of the day, I'd like to hear what you've come up with."

My daughter got a thoughtful look on her face and didn't say anything for a couple minutes. Then she piped up.

"I've got it," she said.

"Got what?" I replied.

"A new name for what you do."

"Already?" I said, skeptically.

"Uh-huh."

"Okay, what is it?"

"Few Appointments, Straight Teeth."

Few Appointments, Straight Teeth—F.A.S.T. I may just be a tad prejudiced, but I think my daughter is brilliant. At the very least, she has a great future in advertising. F.A.S.T. says it all. And this is how it works.

Few Appointments, Straight Teeth

The idea that getting and adjusting braces requires twenty, thirty, or forty appointments over two to five years is kind of baked into the orthodontic process. It's partially a function of the system where patients pay for braces over many years (I'll say more about this in the "How to Pay for It" section of chapter 6), but it's also a function of how traditional braces work. To make adjustments, wires must be changed and bent, and that can only be done in an orthodontist's office. That is not required with clear aligners.

Let me give you some statistics from a study I conducted a short while ago on the time it took to treat patients in my office—the last fifty patients who had traditional braces compared to the last fifty who had clear aligners:

- Traditional braces users averaged twenty-three months to complete the treatment and twenty-two office visits, including two emergency visits.

- Clear aligner users averaged *ten months* to complete the treatment and *eight office visits, and had no emergency visits.*

I should also add that my goal, which I know is achievable, is to get the average time down to *six months* with clear aligners—and possibly as few as *four appointments!* How, you might well ask, is this even possible? How can there be such a huge discrepancy in the amount of time it takes to straighten teeth?

It's all in how the system works. We can do more with your teeth more quickly with clear aligners because the teeth move more easily, faster, and more predictably. And there is no need to come into the office to adjust clear aligners because the custom, computer-modeled sets of aligners define a clear path for the movement of your teeth that only requires you to change sets on the schedule the orthodontist gives you.

A good example of how much more efficient this system is has to do with teeth that don't need to be moved, that are already in the position you want them in when treatment begins. With metal braces, those teeth must move along with all of the other ones. There is no flexibility in the system—the same wire connects and moves all of the teeth, whether they need it or not. So, what does the orthodontist have to do? When the out-of-position teeth get into position, the ones that were in the right position at the beginning have to be moved *back* into the right position as well—which, of course, requires more time. How inefficient is that?

Another factor that makes clear aligners work more quickly are the attachments I described in the previous chapter. Because there are so many different attachment shapes, and because their placement is done with the assistance of a highly accurate computer program, the orthodontist is able to direct the teeth more precisely, which means fewer adjustments to get the teeth into the right position, which means that they get into that position more quickly and easily.

Eating with clear aligners on (or, if you prefer, using the chew toys that are available) also speeds up the movement of teeth "naturally," by exerting pressure on the aligners. I've actually observed a decrease in the time it takes to move teeth for my clear aligner patients who regularly eat with their aligners on.

Rubber bands for correcting the bite are used with braces as well as with clear aligners. With braces it is not typically possible to start using rubber bands until the braces have been on the teeth for six to twelve months. With clear aligners, rubber bands can be started day one. Another huge time saver.

There's also very little to break with clear aligners (occasionally an attachment may come off), so patients using them never lose tooth movement time because a wire or bracket breaks, a situation that temporarily eliminates the pressure on some of the teeth being moved. And, of course, that pressure can't be reintroduced until the patient can make an appointment with the orthodontist—not always an easy thing to do with busy work and school schedules. Breakage is especially frequent for younger children and teenagers, who are much less conscious of the consequences of eating the kinds of foods that cause breakage than adults are.

You can see why clear aligners move teeth faster, with fewer office visits, and no interruptions in the treatment (unless the patient doesn't cooperate, which I'll get into in the next chapter, "What the Patient Needs to Do"). But imagine a system where, during the entire course of your treatment, you never even have to see an orthodontist? Well, that system is here, and I'd like to tell you about that, too.

Virtual Orthodontics Is Good for You

Though you may not have thought about it, there are a lot of "soft costs" associated with orthodontic work, along with the not insignificant amount of cash you put out for the work. Time is certainly the biggest soft cost. Whether you're going to the orthodontist's office yourself or taking a child, the amount of time is significant. You have to take time off of work, wait your turn in the office—and, let's be honest, doctors don't have a great reputation for running on time—and then get back to work/school. You have your gas and the wear-and-tear on your car—or you take public transportation, which can really up the cost in time. On average, it takes three to four hours out of your day to go to the orthodontist. If you have a typical treatment that lasts thirty months and thirty appointments, that is ninety hours spent on those appointments. If you earn $25 per hour that is an additional $2,250 in soft costs associated with the treatment.

Virtual orthodontics almost completely eliminates office visits. While that thought might initially make you uncomfortable, you just need to realize that your orthodontist doesn't do any less work. The difference is that almost all of the work is done up front, through careful, thoughtful calculation on a sophisticated computer program. With this program, we're able to provide a level of precision and predictability in orthodontic treatment that we've never been able to provide before. This is why I referred to it earlier as a revolution in orthodontics.

The final component of having the best possible orthodontic experience is what you, as the patient, do during the course of treatment and after. I'll talk more about what that entails in the next chapter, "What Patients Need to Do."

KEEP THIS IN MIND

- Be clear what you want your orthodontic treatment to accomplish and find an orthodontist who's good at it—and be sure to talk to the orthodontist's patients who've had such treatments.

- Invisalign clear aligners are, hands down, the most sophisticated, effective, and fastest-working aligners in the world when employed by an orthodontist who is an expert in their use.

- Virtual orthodontics is here to stay.

CHAPTER SIX

What Patients Need to Do

A lot of people don't like to hear this, but orthodontic treatment is a team sport. They would rather sit back and put all the responsibility on the doctor—and, certainly, a lot of it belongs there—but the best doctor in the world can't help someone who refuses to do his or her part to make the treatment successful. In this chapter, we're going to talk about the kinds of things you can do to help ensure that your orthodontic treatment, or your child's, is successful.

The other responsibility you have, of course, is to pay for your treatment—you and, with any luck, your dental insurance company. I've already mentioned the way orthodontics is currently tied to a system of monthly payments over a long period of time, and I'll tell you what's wrong with that. I'll also give you a warning or two and talk about a couple ways that you might be able to reduce the cost of your orthodontic work done.

The most basic thing you need to do to make your orthodontic work—of any kind—successful is something you wouldn't think I would have to say—but experience tells me I do—and that is: keep your orthodontic appointments. You'll be amazed to learn that there are people out there who get braces put on their teeth and then disappear. I won't see them for a year. And when I ask them why, they usually say something like, "I was busy."

Okay, you're busy, but you're also paying a lot of money to get your teeth fixed, and they're not going to get fixed if you don't show up and let me adjust your braces—at the very least, it's going to take me a lot longer to finish your treatment, and who in their right mind wants to extend the amount of time they have braces on their teeth? There's that saying, "Showing up is half the battle," and that's certainly true in orthodontics.

Must-Dos with Traditional Braces

Now, let's talk about your part of the bargain—beyond showing up—with traditional metal braces.

MUST-DOS WITH TRADITIONAL BRACES

- *Watch what you eat.*

- *Keep your teeth clean.*

- *If you've had rubber bands prescribed for bite correction purposes, wear them faithfully.*

- *After your treatment is over, wear your retainer.*

First of all, watch what you eat. The metal wire and brackets are vulnerable to any kind of hard or tough food—steak, pizza crust, hard candy, crusty bread, etc.—which requires, at the least, very careful chewing or, at best, abstinence. If you break the wire on your braces, it can stab you painfully in the cheek—and it immediately halts your treatment, until you have time in your busy schedule to get to the orthodontist to put in a new wire. Breaking off a single bracket is equally problematic, because it throws off the tension of the wire on all of the teeth, as well as stopping the movement of the individual tooth with the broken bracket.

If a tooth goes way out of position for either of these reasons, and we've reached a certain stage of treatment—say I've started using the stainless-steel wire with the little bends in it—I can't necessarily stay with it. I've got to go to a softer wire, grab the tooth with that softer wire and move it back into position, and only then go back to my stainless-steel wire. It takes a long time to do that. Patients don't understand that if a bracket breaks off, it's not just a simple thing of putting the bracket back on and we're right back where we were. It means going back a bit and working our way up to where we were again—and that can take several weeks.

So, keep in mind that, *when either of these things happen, it's important to get back to your orthodontist as soon as possible,* so you don't throw off your treatment plan any more or longer than necessary.

Another thing you MUST do is keep your teeth clean. In the United States, thirty months is the average length of an orthodontic treatment. That's two and a half years you're going to have braces on. During that time, it's going to be a lot easier for you to get food caught in your mouth and held against your teeth, which causes cavities. You can get *a lot* of cavities in two and a half years—and that's just over the average amount of time with braces; you could have them for four years or five years. You could do a lot of damage to your teeth—thousands of dollars' worth—if you're not keeping the teeth clean. The orthodontist will try to keep you motivated to keep your teeth clean, but it's you who must clean them, day in and day out.

A diligent orthodontist will tell you that if can't keep your teeth clean, then you're not responsible enough to have braces. In my office, if you can't keep your teeth clean, I take your braces off. I have to protect you from yourself. You can get them back on when you're ready to wear braces *and* keep your teeth clean. At that point, we'll try again.

It's borderline malpractice if an orthodontist leaves braces on a patient who's not keeping the teeth clean. I mentioned the court case where an orthodontist got sued for leaving the braces on when a patient wasn't keeping his teeth clean, because the kid had $10,000 or $15,000 worth of damage to his teeth when his braces came off. If that doesn't scare you enough to keep your teeth clean when you've got braces, I don't know what will.

If your treatment involves using rubber bands along with your braces—and I don't mean the little colored ones on the brackets, I mean the larger ones used to achieve bite correction—then wear your rubber bands. They serve a very important purpose and they're not that hard to wear.

I have a crazy story about that. There's a device called a "non-cooperation bite correction appliance," which takes the place of rubber bands. But this is a significant piece of hardware—bulky, uncomfortable, is cemented onto the teeth, so much more of a pain than the rubber bands. I had a teenager in my office with his father, and I held up this big device and held up the rubber bands and said, "Which one would you rather wear?" A no-brainer, right?

But, no, the kid said, "Just give me the appliance, because I'm never going to wear the rubber bands." Shocked, I look at the father and said, "The appliance is going to cost you a thousand dollars—do you want to pay that?" I was thinking the guy's going to say, "No way." But, instead, he said, "Well, if he won't wear the rubber bands … " So we put the appliance in. Go figure.

So, if you don't want to wear rubber bands, you can have that appliance in your mouth, *but if you do have rubber bands, wear them.*

Finally, once your treatment is done, you'll be given a retainer, which does exactly what the name indicates it will do: it retains the beautiful positions of your teeth that you and your orthodontist worked all those years to achieve. *Wear your retainer*—ideally, for some amount of time every day for the rest of your life. Otherwise, your teeth are going to move and shift around, because, as we age, our bodies change. Nobody in his forties looks the same way he did in his twenties. And the teeth are part of the body, so you can't expect them to stay perfectly aligned over time without some help, and that's what a retainer provides. Wearing your retainer is a simple, cost-effective way to keep your teeth beautiful for the rest of your life. I am working on developing the whole-body retainer. Get a mold of yourself at, say, age twenty-one, and then sleep in it every night so you stay looking twenty-one forever. A guaranteed best seller!

Must-Dos with Invisalign Braces

As you've probably guessed already, the list of must-dos with Invisalign clear aligners is simpler than the list for traditional braces. You'll have very few office appointments, so you don't need to worry about finding the time to go. You don't need to worry about what you eat, because you can't break clear aligners. And you don't need to worry about food getting caught in them, because (a) they fit snuggly (b), you can rinse them off easily in a few seconds, and (c) you can take them out and easily brush and floss just like you did before you started treatment.

MUST-DOS WITH INVISALIGN BRACES

The few things you need to do with Invisalign clear aligners are:

- *Switch to the next set of aligners on the schedule given you by your orthodontist.*

- *If you've had rubber bands for bite correction, wear them faithfully.*

- *After your treatment is over, wear your retainer.*

- *Brush and floss as normal.*

There's not much to say about changing your aligners in a timely manner, except that it's just as important as seeing your orthodontist with traditional braces. Your orthodontist can't move your teeth properly if you don't show up to have your wire adjusted, and Invisalign clear aligners can't move your teeth properly if you don't use them in the sequence and with the timing that's been planned for you.

That's it, for both kinds of braces, and, while you need to be significantly more vigilant with traditional braces, none of these requirements is oppressive. Yet, so many people neglect some or all of them—to the detriment of their orthodontic treatment and the overall health of their teeth. I'll repeat what I said at the beginning of this chapter: orthodontics is a team sport. Orthodontists can't win the game alone. We need your help.

How to Pay for It

It's time for another one of my pet peeves: the way orthodontists have their patients pay for treatment. The traditional model when paying for braces is to have the patient put 25 percent down and then pay the balance with monthly payments over two, three, or four years—depending on what kind of monthly payment the patient can afford. Some patients try to extend their payments out for as long as they can, so their monthly payments are as low as possible.

There is nothing inherently wrong with this setup, but it's the way orthodontists respond to this approach that causes the problem. What happens is, if the patient's payments will be going for thirty-six months, then the treatment will take thirty-six months. If the payments will come in over twenty-four months, then the treatment now magically takes only twenty-four months. The reason this happens is that orthodontists don't want to take the braces off until the patient is done paying for the treatment. They're afraid that if they take the braces off before the patient is done paying, then the patient will conveniently forget to make the monthly payments.

I recently hired a couple of orthodontic assistants who, when I told them about this approach, both said they knew that the orthodontists they worked for were fudging treatments, often doing nothing, or next to nothing, at a given appointment to keep their patients coming into the office for a longer period of time. This does not demonstrate a lot of trust for patients. It also artificially increases the amount of time treatments take and all of the inherent danger for decay, root shortening, and inconvenience by increasing the number of appointments.

There are a lot of big corporate dental/orthodontic offices that advertise a low monthly payment for their braces. But what they don't advertise is a total fee for the braces. For example, they'll say, "Get your braces for $99 a month." And people think, "Wow, I can afford $99 a month," and they feel good, because they know that their neighbor down the street is paying $150 or $200 a month. So, $99 a month sounds great.

They go to the orthodontist at one of these offices, who claims that they're going to get little Gloria's braces on and off as quickly as possible. There is either no down payment or a minimal down payment, maybe another $100 or $200. But they don't call them down payments, they call them start fees. I'm not really sure how a start fee is different from a down payment, but they'd like you to think it is.

Then the patient or the parent asks how long the treatment is going to last, and these companies typically say it's two to two and a half years on average. They say they never really know for sure in advance, because it depends on various factors. Then comes the part they don't tell you about; they nickel-and-dime you to death. If you have broken brackets—which you now know is going to happen regularly—they charge you anywhere from $35–$50 for every broken bracket. If you miss an appointment, there can be a $100 fee for that.

And then—and this is the big thing—for some reason, they can never seem to get done in the "average" two to two-and-a-half years. It almost always takes three or four years. I've spoken to patients who have been at these practices, and they say the patients only see the doctor every other appointment and most of the time all they do is change those little colored elastic ties that hold the wires onto the brackets. The doctor doesn't even adjust the braces; they just change the elastics.

But the patients don't know how braces work, of course, so they just go along and, all of a sudden, they're at forty-eight months times $99 a month, so they've shelled out $4,800 dollars plus all the extra fees! They're paying $5,000 or $6,000 for the braces—and then, on top of that, there's an extra fee for the retainers at the end. They end up paying the same or more than they would have paid at a traditional orthodontic office.

This is something that you need to be aware of when you talk to an orthodontist. You need to ask how do you pay for the orthodontic treatment. You need to ask how payments relate to the length of your treatment. You need to ask what happens if your treatment is finished before you're done paying. You need to ask if your treatment will be done sooner if you pay up front. Those are the questions you need to ask any orthodontist, to get clarity on whether or not your payment schedule relates to the length of your treatment.

One of the reasons that I can confidently complete treatments within such a short time is that I'm not worrying about getting monthly payments. I have a patient finance service called Care Credit that pays me up front and my patients pay that service on a monthly basis. This is a much cleaner setup that allows me to put my focus where it belongs—on getting my patients' treatments done as quickly as possible. I also give my clients discounts for paying up front. The point is to get treatments to work faster, not scheme about how to drag them out. These two policies alone, if universally adopted, would speed up orthodontic work in every practice in the country.

If you want to get your orthodontic treatment done as fast as possible, you should find a way to pay for your orthodontic treatment up front. Then you need to get after the orthodontist constantly, reminding him/her that you want your braces off as quickly as possible, and asking for an estimate of how much longer it will take. Orthodontists usually have a reasonable guesstimate of this; they just don't want to tell you—especially if you're paying monthly over a long period of time.

WHAT YOU MIGHT NOT KNOW
ABOUT INSURANCE

Everyone wants their dental insurance to pay for orthodontic treatment, of course, but, in my opinion, insurance companies are somewhat unscrupulous about how they explain to patients what and how they pay. Insurance companies tell patients that their orthodontic insurance will cover half of the orthodontic fee up to a maximum of $1,500–$2,000. Well, orthodontic fees in the United States run $5,000 to $7,000, so a $1,500 benefit doesn't get you anywhere near half of that fee.

But that's how they put it, saying they pay for half of a treatment up to a max of $1,500—which really comes out to about *one-fifth* of the treatment cost. They say it's a half, but if they can find a traditional orthodontic office that will do braces for $3,000 in today's market, that would be nothing short of a miracle. In a traditional orthodontic office, that kind of fee simply doesn't exist. Also, the $1,500 is usually a lifetime maximum, so you're "one and done." The only way you would ever get more would be if you or your employer changed insurance companies.

Please be aware that *your orthodontist does not determine your benefits.* Your doctor has absolutely no control over the size of the orthodontic benefits any insurance company offers. Patients sometimes ask me why I don't make the insurance company pay more for whatever work the patient is having done, but, to put it bluntly, the insurance company doesn't really care what I think they should pay. Yes, we interact with them on your behalf, but it's really just a service that orthodontic offices submit your claims for you. We have no clout with the insurance companies.

Here's another thing you probably know little about—how insurance companies pay out. Orthodontists don't get the payment in a lump sum; it's doled out to us over twelve to twenty-four months. If you get that $1,500 benefit toward the cost of your braces, the insurance company will pay it out to the doctor in small portions—perhaps $50 to $100 per month, perhaps quarterly or even once per year. Get this, the insurance company won't even tell us how they are going to pay us. We just have to wait and see how they decide to pay. It is also common that we have to be on hold with the insurance company for forty-five minutes to help you get your benefit, and then after holding for that long they hang up on us and we have to start the process all over again. This is normal business for the insurance companies. It is unbelievable the ways they come up with to hold on to your premium dollars. This is a huge benefit that doctors do for their patients.

And here's the real kicker: if you drop or lose your insurance at *any* point during the period your insurance company is making these payments to your orthodontist, *the payments stop immediately and you have to pay the remaining insurance balance yourself.* Seems incredibly unfair after the insurance company committed to paying that portion of the cost, but that's how it is. More than one of my patients has had a rude awakening when they got a bill for the balance they thought the insurance company had paid.

Another thing: when you get new insurance you sometimes have to wait for a year before you can use any of the orthodontic coverage. You can't just sign up and go get treatment.

Before you buy orthodontic insurance, it's a good idea to go to an orthodontist first and get a consult—preferably the orthodontist you might use to do the work. Find out how much braces are going to cost at that orthodontist, and find out all their payment plans, then start shopping around for the best combination of premiums and coverage you can find.

The other thing that can work well for patients is to take advantage of their flexible spending account or health savings account, if they have one of those at work. Those enable you to accumulate untaxed money and use that to pay for healthcare. In our office, we really bend over backward to help people maximize those kinds of accounts—and any orthodontic office you work with should be willing to do the same. We will let patients make annual payments to us from those accounts, so they don't have the hassle of monthly payments. In January, or whenever their fiscal year ends, when they get all of their FSA or HSA money, then they just make one big payment to us from the account. We spread payments out over two or three different years for them, so they can pay all of their orthodontic costs with pretax dollars, which is huge savings for a lot of people.

Another way we help people out is by giving them a 10 percent discount if they pay the entire cost of treatment they're getting, up front. On $5,000 braces, if the insurance company pays $1,500, that leaves $3,500 for the patient to pay, so they get a $350 break from us on top of that, which is a significant sum of money.

Orthodontic insurance is helpful, to some extent, as are HSAs and FSAs, and then there is third-party financing. Care Credit is probably the single largest company that does medical procedure financing for consumers. It's through Care Credit, as I mentioned above, that I get my payment in full, up front, and the patient pays them on a monthly basis. They can get up to sixty months to pay. Lending Point is another such company that is coming on strong.

If you or your child really needs orthodontic work, there are creative ways to get help paying for it. Often, kids' grandparents are often willing to help out, or it can be part of birthday or holiday gift for a child. Other relatives might be able to help out, as well. A lot of people like home equity loans, because they get a tax break on those as well as getting the money they need for the orthodontic work.

In the next chapter, I'll talk about *why*—objectively speaking—it's important to get orthodontic work done. It can change your, or your child's, life.

KEEP THIS IN MIND

- Orthodontics is a team sport. If you want your traditional braces to work, then you need to:

- Watch what you eat.

- Keep your teeth clean.

- If you've had rubber bands put in your mouth for bite correction purposes, wear them faithfully.

- After your treatment is over, wear your retainer.

- With Invisalign clear aligners there's a lot less to worry about—no breakage causing delays in treatment, no tooth decay from trapped food, but you do have to put in your new aligners on schedule and keep them in (along with rubber bands, if your treatment calls for them).

- Understand what your orthodontic insurance will pay for treatment (it's usually not more than $1,500 or so), how they'll make payments to your orthodontist (so you aren't surprised if you lose the insurance and have to pay the balance), and find creative ways to finance what's not covered (FSAs, HSAs, home equity loans, loans from relatives, etc.).

CHAPTER SEVEN

Good Teeth Are Key to Success and Happiness—Really!

T here are many functional reasons for getting orthodontic treatments, but many people have the work done simply because they want to look good. I recently did a Google search about how looking good brings greater success and I got no fewer than 24 million results! Clearly, this is on people's minds. Most of us have a visceral negative reaction when we see bad teeth, so it's understandable that people would be concerned about how their own teeth look.

We all want to look our best, because we feel more confident if we're looking our best. How our teeth look is key to that, because people look at our face when they talk to us, and, anytime we smile, there those teeth are. It turns out that smiling is important, too, and I'll get

We all want to look our best, because we feel more confident if we're looking our best. How our teeth look is key to that.

into that as well. You can smile in any language and make a connection. But if your teeth don't look good, then you're more likely to suppress your smile than use it to make that connection.

How you look even has financial repercussions. In his 2011 book *Beauty Pays: Why Attractive People Are More Successful,* Daniel Hamermesh, an economist formerly at the University of Texas in Austin, demonstrates that there is a clear economic reward for looking our best.

Other research has shown that people who smile a lot—as evidenced by photos of them taken over their lifetime—are happier and more successful than are people who don't smile much.[1] Now, this stands to reason, but what we don't know about the latter group is *why* they don't smile more. For a significant number of people, it's simply because they don't like the way their teeth look—and orthodontic treatment can do something about that.

That's one of the great things about being an orthodontist, working with people like that and seeing the change that happens after we've done our work. I've had lots of patients whose personalities just blossomed after they get their teeth straightened or a missing tooth replaced or any other kind of orthodontics that improves their appearance. It really changes their personality; you can see that they're enjoying their life more, because they're happier, and that makes them more enjoyable to be around.

I've heard from people's spouses how much better these people's relationships are with everyone in the family and at work. They start being more successful, or they switch careers—whether to make more money or just to get into something they've always wanted

---

1   Meg Selig, "The 9 Superpowers of Your Smile," *Psychology Today*, May 25, 2016, https://www.psychologytoday.com/us/blog/changepower/201605/the-9-superpowers-your-smile.

to get into—because they finally have the confidence to do it. It's amazing the ripple effect that having your teeth fixed can have.

There are a number of studies that demonstrate the effects of orthodontic work on people's lives.

Having healthy teeth doesn't just help you socially, it also affects your overall health. There's lots of research coming out, now, that links gum disease, which is basically gingivitis, and periodontal disease with increased risk of heart disease, type 2 diabetes, respiratory disease, kidney disease, and even fertility problems in women.[2] In 2009, the *Journal of Obstetrics and Gynecology* published a report that said when women don't have healthy mouths, it takes them two months longer to conceive than it does women with healthy mouths. So, it's not all just about appearance, it's about good health!

> *Having healthy teeth doesn't just help you socially, it also affects your overall health.*

Orthodontic work *ought* to pay off, because it's expensive! I talked about the hard and soft costs in the previous chapter—it's a major investment of time and money. So, it's reassuring to know that there can be significant financial, social, and health rewards for having orthodontic work done.

I have to share a story here about the flip side of having orthodontic work done, the unexpected "negative" consequences of having better teeth. One of my patients is a sheriff's deputy, a great guy, who had pretty messed-up teeth. He actually looked kind of scary. We did the work on his teeth, and he *loved* the results—he was

---

2 "Periodontal Disease and Systemic Health," American Academy of Periodontology, https://www.perio.org/consumer/gum-disease-and-other-diseases; Catharine Paddock, "Women's Fertility Linked To Oral Health," Medical News Today, July 6, 2011, https://www.medicalnewstoday.com/articles/230568.php.

definitely one of those people who became happier because of having orthodontic work done.

But, one day, he came in and said, "You know I'm a sheriff's deputy, right, Doc?"

I said I did.

"And you know I really like the way my teeth look, right?"

Again, I said I did.

"Well, I have to tell you one thing I've noticed since I got my teeth straightened that's not so great. My 'clients' have started resisting arrest a lot more."

"Oh," I said, "so, you don't look as scary as you used to, huh?"

"Apparently not!"

Then moral of the story: Maybe if you're a cop or a bounty hunter or a professional wrestler—something where nasty looks are sort of an advantage—you might want to think twice about getting your teeth fixed. (Although your girlfriend or wife might want to weigh in on that.)

Speaking of wives and girlfriends and their relationships, that's another pet peeve of mine. I hear things like this all the time from married men who don't want to be bothered with having their teeth straightened: "I don't need to look good or be healthy—I'm married." What a horrible attitude. I think it's sad that so many men are apathetic about how they look to their wife and family. It's no wonder the divorce rate is so high. I can't help wonder if this has anything to do with them being taken for granted by their husbands.

Another funny thing is that, after a divorce, both people in the ex-couple do things such as joining a health club, eating better, getting orthodontic treatments or cosmetic surgery to improve their appearance, and so on, so they can meet someone of the opposite sex, and yes, get married all over again. If they'd put a little more of that effort in during their marriage, including trying to stay attractive, then maybe they wouldn't have gotten divorced in the first place!

KEEP THIS IN MIND

- If your teeth look good, then you'll smile more and look better, and statistics show that people who smile more and look good are more successful socially and financially.

- Medical studies show that a healthy mouth also affects your overall health, from your respiratory system to your reproductive system.

- It's worth looking your best not only for people in your public life but also for your girlfriend/boyfriend/spouse—looking better for them might help avoid a relationship coming to a bad end.

The Dos and Don'ts of Orthodontics

The purpose of this book is to arm you with enough information to choose an orthodontist wisely and have the best possible experience you can have with orthodontic treatment. This has required me to debunk a lot of misinformation about orthodontics—some of it perpetuated by orthodontists themselves, who are not likely to be happy with what I've done. But this book is not for them; it's for you, the patient. You pay a lot of money for orthodontic services, and you should not have to take on that expense without being clear about what's involved, medically and financially.

You pay a lot of money for orthodontic services, and you should not have to take on that expense without being clear about what's involved, medically and financially.

You may have noticed that I'm a huge fan of Invisalign. But I am not a spokesperson for the company; I am not paid to endorse them; I get no more benefit from using their system than any other orthodontist gets. The reason I am so enthusiastic about the Invisalign system is because it has enabled me to do revolutionary things for my patients. I'm a big fan of Invisalign because it works well in the hands of an experienced doctor. End of story.

We've covered a lot of ground in this book, so I've put together this handy list of dos and don'ts that covers all of the major points I've made about how to choose an orthodontist and get the best orthodontic experience.

DOS

- Do interview any orthodontist you're considering to do work on yourself or your child, using the information you've learned in this book. Getting multiple opinions is a good idea.

- Do be clear what you want your orthodontic treatment to accomplish and find an orthodontist who's good at it— and be sure to talk to the orthodontist's patients who've had such treatments.

- Do keep in mind, when vetting an orthodontist, that straightening teeth is just one aspect of orthodontic health; it needs to be balanced with consideration of the jaw joint (TMJ) and bite.

- Do know the advantages of clear aligners before choosing traditional metal braces: there are no parts to break; food is less likely to get caught behind them, and they can be rinsed immediately if it does; they're comfortable and not obtrusive visually; treatment can take as few as six months.

- Do go to an orthodontist who is very skilled with Invisalign, because the Invisalign system gives the best results in the shortest amount of time, with the least discomfort and the lowest overall cost. But, you must find an orthodontist with lots of experience. If you hear from them, "We may need to put braces on to get a good result," they do not have the experience and confidence to do a great job for you.

- Do keep in mind that orthodontics is a team sport. If you want traditional braces to work, you need to:

  □ Watch what you eat.

  □ Keep your teeth clean.

  □ If you had rubber bands prescribed for bite correction, wear them faithfully.

  □ After your treatment is over, wear your retainer.

- Do keep in mind that with Invisalign there's a lot less to worry about—no breakage causing delays in treatment, no tooth decay from trapped food, but you do have to put in your new aligners on schedule and keep them in (along with rubber bands, if your treatment calls for them).

- Do understand what your orthodontic insurance will pay for (it's usually not more than $1,500–$2,000 or so), how they'll make payments to your orthodontist (so you aren't surprised if you lose the insurance and have to pay the balance), and find creative ways to finance what's not covered (FSAs, HSAs, home equity loans, loans from relatives, etc.).

DON'TS

- Don't rely on the diploma of an orthodontist to tell you how skilled and dedicated he/she is—the graduate who squeaks by gets the same diploma as the one who worked hard and graduated at the top of the class.

- Don't go to orthodontists who do expensive procedures that have not been proven effective—especially ones who want to put braces on children at a young age without explaining the real need and benefit. Always remember if you do orthodontic treatment when there are still half of the baby teeth you will most likely be paying for another set to finish the job after all of the permanent teeth have erupted.

- Don't assume you need to get traditional braces; they require a lot of time, discomfort, and expense that is no longer necessary.

- Don't get orthodontic work on primary (baby) teeth or children's jaws unless necessary for some extreme reason— and know that such work won't typically eliminate the need for second round of orthodontic work (called phase two) once the permanent teeth erupt.

- Don't let your dentist or orthodontist do work in your child's mouth for sleep apnea without first getting a medical diagnosis for the condition as well as follow-up studies to prove the success of the proposed treatment. Otherwise, some other types of treatment may need to still be done.

- Don't think of orthodontic work as something done for cosmetic reasons only. It is done for functional reasons to correct problems with the bite and TMJ as well.

- If your teeth look good, then you'll smile more and look better, and statistics show that people who smile more and look good are more successful socially and financially. People with straighter teeth and healthier mouths overall are healthier and happier.

- Don't think it's not worth having your teeth done to look your best for your girlfriend/boyfriend/spouse—looking better for them might help avoid a relationship coming to a bad end, which is way more expensive than orthodontic treatment.

My Approach to Orthodontics

I hope you have learned a lot about how I practice orthodontics by reading this book, but now I'd like to focus on how we work to make our patients' orthodontic experience the best possible one. My practice, called Trinity Orthodontics (trinityorthodontics.com), currently has two locations in the Denver, Colorado, metro area. They are in Thornton and Arvada.

The first principle we operate on is total honesty with our patients. We never prescribe orthodontic treatment that isn't necessary, and we try to give our patients all the information they need to make a decision about whether or not to have a treatment done—and, if they decide to have it, how we'll go about it. We inform patients about the cost of treatments up front, and try to make it as convenient and economical to pay for treatments as we can. We also encourage any prospective patients to talk with our current patients to get the real scoop on what working with us is like.

> *The first principle we operate on is total honesty with our patients.*

One of our basic operating principles is KISS: Keep It Super Simple. There was a man named Deming, who did a lot of work with Toyota to make their productivity amazing and high quality, and simplicity was an important part of that. I like to boil everything we do in our practice down to the absolutely simplest approach, because that's usually what's going to be the most efficient approach and is going to yield the best results. Humans in general tend to overly complicate things, and I think orthodontists are particularly good at it, so we make a conscious effort in our practice to get away from that, to make things clear and simple for our patients.

I've already told you about our F.A.S.T. approach—and about my young daughter coming up with the name. F.A.S.T. stands for Few Appointments, Straight Teeth. We use Invisalign mostly in our F.A.S.T. system, because it's an approach where all the tooth movements are preprogrammed on the computer, so we don't have to see patients all the time to adjust the appliance, as we do with traditional braces. We design your entire treatment plan on the computer, ahead of time, so all the "adjusting" gets done each time you put in a new set of aligners. That's where the Few Appointments comes in. Straight Teeth refers to the fact that the Invisalign technology gives you beautifully aligned teeth more quickly and comfortably than any other approach can possibly do. I am also an expert in correcting TMJ problems as well as complex bite issues.

Approaches such as our F.A.S.T. system are really game changers for patients. Tele-dentistry is going to make it possible for orthodontists to do consultations over the Internet, so patients don't have to go into the doctor's office and spend hours waiting. We are already developing these systems in our current practice and patients love the convenience.

Ultimately, at Trinity Orthodontics, it's about having everything up front and honest and forthright. That's our guarantee.

Our Services

Custom designed braces

Invisalign

TMJ problems

Bite problems

Snoring and sleep apnea treatment

CPSIA information can be obtained
at www.ICGtesting.com
Printed in the USA
BVHW041311181219
567049BV00006B/43/P

9 781642 250459